635
JO   Johnson, Sylvia A.
       Potatoes

DATE			
Jan.	10	1995	Ashley

© THE BAKER & TAYLOR CO.

POTATOES

POTATOES

by Sylvia A. Johnson

Photographs by Masaharu Suzuki

A Lerner Natural Science Book

Lerner Publications Company • Minneapolis

Sylvia A. Johnson, Series Editor

Translation of original text by Hiroko and Joseph McDermott

The publisher wishes to thank Hugh J. Murphy, Professor of Agronomy, University of Maine, and past president of the Potato Association of America, for his assistance in the preparation of this book.

Additional photographs courtesy of: p. 7, Charlton Photos; pp. 13, 16, 40, Kenneth Chapman, Maine Cooperative Extension Service; pp. 14 (top), 15, James F. Dill, Maine Cooperative Extension Service; p. 39 (top), Ryan Farms, East Grand Forks, Minnesota; pp. 39 (bottom), 41, 42, Red River Valley Potato Growers Association. Drawings on pages 20 and 23 by Kayo Takechi.

The glossary on page 46 gives definitions and pronunciations of words shown in **bold type** in the text.

LIBRARY OF CONGRESS CATALOGING IN PUBLICATION DATA

Johnson, Sylvia A.
    Potatoes.

        (A Lerner Natural Science Book)
        Adaptation of: Jagaimo / by Masaharu Suzuki.
        Includes index.
        Summary: Describes the development of the potato, including information on planting seed potatoes, sprouting, the growth of the plant and its underground tubers, and the role played by tubers in the life of the potato plant.
        1. Potatoes—Juvenile literature. [1. Potatoes]
    I. Suzuki, Masaharu, ill. II. Suzuki, Masaharu.
    Jagaimo. III. Series.
    SB211.P8J63 1984   635'.21   84-5760
    ISBN 0-8225-1459-1 (lib. bdg.)

International Standard Book Number: 0-8225-1459-1
Library of Congress Catalog Number: 84-5760

    2 3 4 5 6 7 8 9 10 91 90 89 88 87 86 85

Have you eaten a potato today? If you are like many people who live in North America and Europe, potatoes may be included in your diet several times a week. The popular potato appears on dinner tables in a great variety of forms—baked, boiled, mashed, french-fried, served in soups and stews, or made into crispy chips. This versatile vegetable is also used as animal feed and as raw material for flour and some kinds of alcoholic beverages.

Just what kind of vegetable is the potato and how does it grow? These questions and others will be answered in the following pages.

Seed potatoes are often cut into pieces before they are planted. In order to grow, each piece must contain a potato "eye."

If you have ever helped to plant potatoes in a backyard garden, you know that they go into the ground in a form different from other common kinds of vegetables. Peas, beans, carrots, squash, and many other garden vegetables are planted as seeds, tiny kernels containing all the parts necessary to produce new plants. Vegetables like tomatoes and peppers are often started as young plants already bearing green leaves. In order to grow rows of healthy potato plants, gardeners bury potatoes in their soil.

Potatoes planted in this way are usually called **seed potatoes** or seedpieces, but the names are misleading. A potato is not a very large seed, nor does it contain seeds. Like a seed, however, it does include all the elements needed to grow a new plant.

Commercial potato growers use large mechanical planters that can plant several rows of seed potatoes at one time. In North America, planting may take place as early as November or as late as June, depending on the climate of the region.

Each potato eye (above) contains several tiny buds (below) that can develop into sprouts.

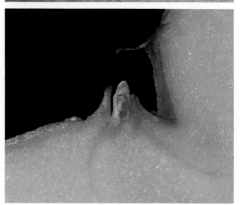

Just how does a seed potato produce a new potato plant? You can observe the beginning of this amazing development right in your own home, with an ordinary potato that was purchased from the supermarket.

Potatoes that have been stored too long or not given the proper treatment will often begin to sprout. If you have such a potato, you can see the fat whitish sprouts growing from its skin.

If you look at a sprouting potato closely, you will notice that the sprouts grow only from certain spots. They emerge only from the **eyes**, the small indentations scattered over the surface of the potato. Located in each eye are several tiny **buds**. These are the parts of the seed potato that produce sprouts. The sprouts in turn will develop into the stems of a new potato plant.

8

Above: A developing potato sprout has a cluster of tiny folded leaves at its tip. From its base grow long, thread-like roots. *Right:* This seed potato has developed in the soil for several weeks. Its sprouts and roots are about four inches (10 centimeters) long.

A potato root begins its development.

The roots of the new plant develop not from the seed potato itself but from the sprouts. At first they grow out in a horizontal direction from the base of the sprouts. Later they will grow from the upper part of the sprout as well.

As you can see in the photographs above and on the opposite page, the roots are covered with fine hairs. When the potato plant is more fully developed, the root hairs will take in water and minerals from the soil. These materials will be used to produce food for the plant's growth. During the early stage of its development, the new plant receives most of its nourishment from nutrients stored in the seed potato.

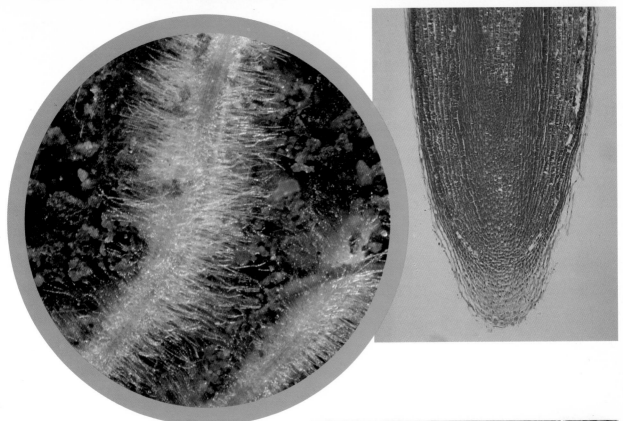

Above left: Potato roots covered with fine root hairs. *Above right:* This photograph, taken through a microscope, shows the delicate tip of a potato root. It is covered by a tiny rootcap that protects the growing end of the root.

Right: This seed potato has been uncovered after growing in the soil for almost a month. Green leaves have already developed on the tips of some of its sprouts.

Two to four weeks after the seed potatoes were put into the ground, the new potato plants are ready to emerge. Their already formed leaves begin to poke through the top layer of soil. Soon the potato field is covered with neat rows of graceful young plants.

This grower is using a cultivator to build up hills of soil around his potato plants.

When the potato plants begin their development, growers have a lot of work to do. They must cultivate their fields to make sure that weeds don't take hold and interfere with the growth of the young plants. Cultivating equipment is also used to build up low hills of soil around the bases of the plants. "Hilling" protects the underground sections of the plant stems, which, as we shall see, are very important parts of potato plants.

Finally, growers may have to spray their fields with insecticides and other chemicals that protect the growing plants from damaging insects and diseases.

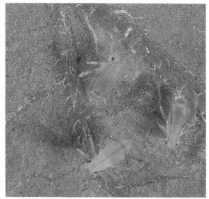

Aphids (above) are tiny sucking insects that feed on potato plants (below).

There are many different kinds of insects that attack potato plants. Aphids, leafhoppers, and other sucking insects use their sharp mouthparts to pierce stems and suck out fluids. These insects not only damage plants by feeding on them but also spread viruses that cause disease.

In North America, the Colorado potato beetle is the insect most feared by potato growers. This small striped beetle eats the leaves of potato plants both in its larval stage and as an adult. If potato beetles are not controlled, they can cause tremendous damage, reducing a field of potato plants to bare stems.

Potato plants are also subject to various kinds of fungus diseases. Potato blight is caused by a fungal growth that attacks plant leaves and stems. The terrible Potato Famine that occurred in Europe during the 1800s was brought about by an epidemic of late blight that destroyed potato crops. Between 1845 and 1847, about 750,000 people in Ireland died of starvation and disease as a result of this devastating crop loss.

14

In spring, adult Colorado potato beetles (upper left) lay their eggs on potato plants. The fat larvae that hatch from the eggs (upper right) feed on the plant leaves, doing tremendous damage. Some growers control potato beetles by hand-picking both larvae and adults (left) from the plants and destroying them.

Late blight is a fungal disease that attacks and kills the leaves (left) and stems (right) of potato plants.

Spraying with insecticides and fungicides helps to protect potato plants from destructive insects and fungal diseases like late blight.

16

A potato plant's compound leaves are arranged in a spiral pattern around the plant stem. This arrangement allows each leaf to get as much sunlight as possible.

Potato plants that are not attacked by disease or insects will develop a healthy growth of bright green leaves. Potato leaves have a rather complicated structure compared to the simple leaves of geranium plants or elm trees. They are known as **compound leaves** because each is made up of small individual sections called **leaflets.** The leaflets grow along thin stalks that are attached to the stems of the plant.

A potato plant's leaves are arranged in a special way around the stems to make sure that each leaf receives as much sunlight as possible. As you can see in the photograph above, the leaves are positioned in a kind of spiral pattern. This arrangement keeps the leaves at the top of the plant from shading the ones below. In this way, each leaf is able to get its share of the precious sunlight that makes the life of the plant possible.

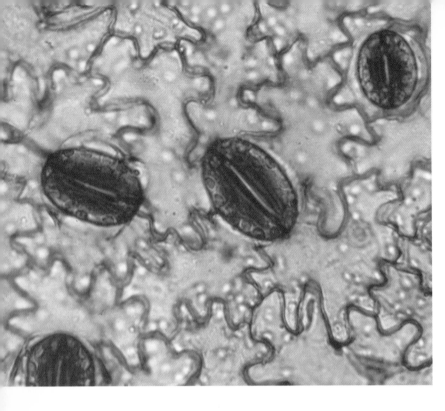

A photograph taken through a microscope showing the pores or stomata in a potato leaf. Each stoma consists of a slit-like opening surrounded by two guard cells.

Sunlight is the energy source that provides fuel for the potato plant's food-producing system. Like all green plants, a potato plant makes food through the process of **photosynthesis**. This word literally means "putting together with light," and that is exactly what a plant does. It produces food by using the energy of the sun to combine raw materials drawn from the soil and from the air.

The basic ingredients that a plant needs for photosynthesis are carbon dioxide, water, and, of course, sunlight. Carbon dioxide is a gas given off by living things during the process of respiration. It is taken into a plant's leaves through tiny openings or pores called **stomata**. The other essential ingredient, water, is drawn up from the soil through the roots.

18

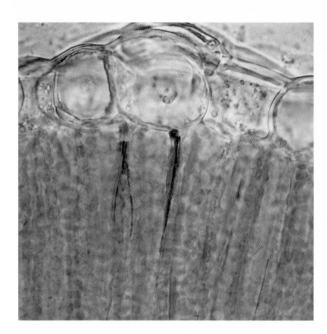

This photograph shows a section of the surface of a potato leaf. The colorless cells of the upper epidermis form the top layer of the leaf. Below are long, thin palisade cells filled with green chloroplasts.

The combining of water and carbon dioxide to form food requires a complex chemical process that takes place in the cells of a plant's leaves. Within these cells are tiny bodies called **chloroplasts,** containing the green pigment **chlorophyll.** Chlorophyll is the material that gives plants their green color, but it also plays a vital role in photosynthesis.

By absorbing sunlight, chlorophyll produces the energy that breaks down and then combines the molecules of water and carbon dioxide. The results of this synthesis are two new substances—oxygen and a form of sugar known as **glucose.**

Glucose is the basic food used by a plant in growing, reproducing, and carrying on all of its life processes. The plant also uses some oxygen, but most of this gas is released through the stomata into the atmosphere. Here it supplies the essential element for the respiration of all forms of animal life, including human beings.

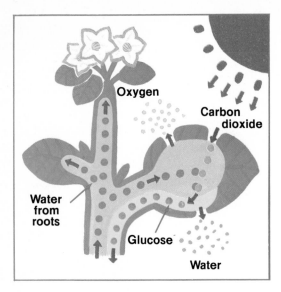

The process of photosynthesis uses the energy of the sun to make glucose out of carbon dioxide and water. Excess water and oxygen, a by-product of photosynthesis, are released through the plant's stomata.

The leaves are the potato plant's primary food-producing centers. The stem contains the transportation system that brings raw materials to the leaves and carries away the finished products of photosynthesis.

This transportation system is made up of tiny tubes or veins arranged in groups. The collections of veins are called **vascular bundles,** and they run up and down the length of the stem, near its outside surface. Together the vascular bundles form a kind of ring, which can be seen in the cross-section of a potato plant's stem shown on the opposite page.

Some of the veins in the vascular bundles carry the water needed for photosynthesis from the roots to the plant's leaves. Minerals taken from the soil are also brought from the roots to the leaves, where they are used in some chemical processes. Other veins in the vascular bundles carry the glucose produced in the leaves to all parts of the plant, where it is used to nourish and sustain life.

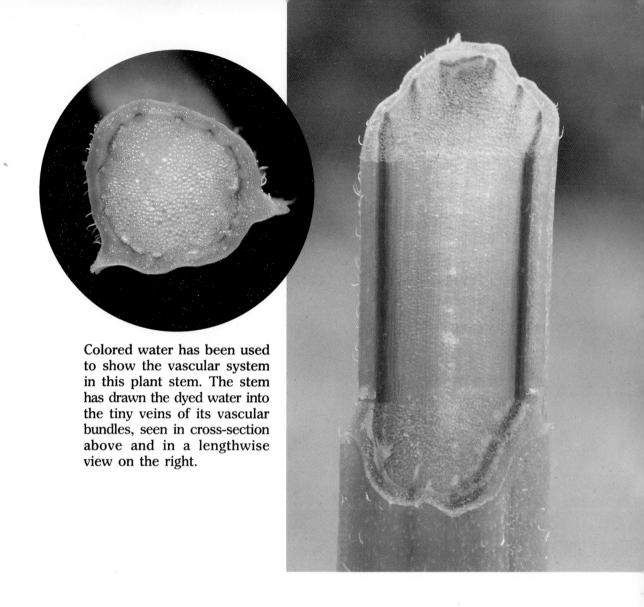

Colored water has been used to show the vascular system in this plant stem. The stem has drawn the dyed water into the tiny veins of its vascular bundles, seen in cross-section above and in a lengthwise view on the right.

The stem of a potato plant has some special features not found in the stems of most other green plants. One such feature is an underground extension called a **rhizome**. The rhizome of a potato plant looks something like a root, but it is actually a special structure designed for food storage.

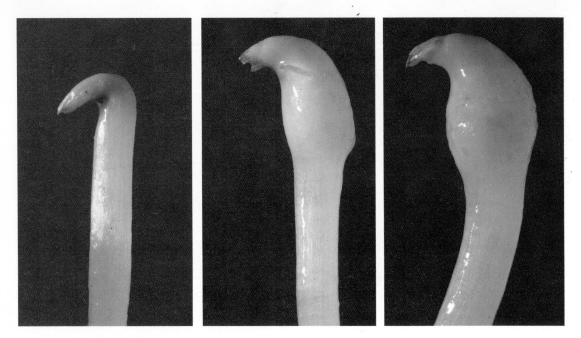

Above and opposite: The tip of a rhizome gradually enlarges as a young tuber is formed.

After a potato plant has finished its initial period of growth, its leaves usually produce more glucose than is needed for the immediate use of the plant. This extra glucose is stored in the form of **starch,** a substance made up of molecules of glucose.

The starch is sent down from the leaves through the vascular system to the rhizomes hidden under the ground. As more and more starch accumulates in a rhizome, it begins to swell at its tip. Eventually a large **tuber** develops at the end of each rhizome. The tubers of a potato plant are what we call potatoes, the nourishing vegetables that have become such an important part of the human diet.

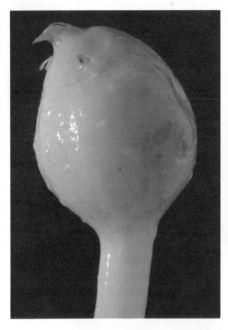

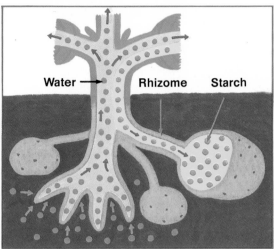

The tubers of a potato plant serve as a storage place for starch.

In this photograph, you can see the tiny white tubers at the ends of the rhizomes, the many fine roots, and the seed potato from which the plant originally developed.

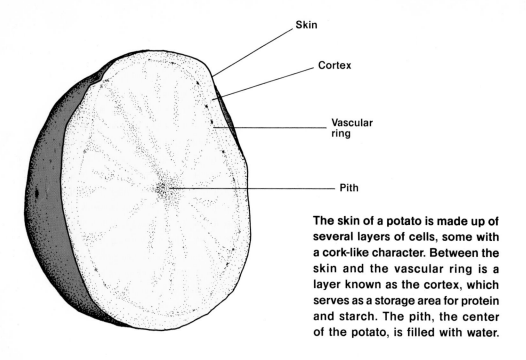

Skin

Cortex

Vascular
ring

Pith

The skin of a potato is made up of several layers of cells, some with a cork-like character. Between the skin and the vascular ring is a layer known as the cortex, which serves as a storage area for protein and starch. The pith, the center of the potato, is filled with water.

The starch in a tuber is transported by a vascular system very much like the system of veins in a plant stem. This is not surprising since a potato tuber is actually an extension of the stem and shares many of its characteristics.

As you can see in the photographs on the opposite page, a potato's vascular system is located near its outer surface. In a cross-section, it appears as a ring, called the **vascular ring.** Starch sent from the leaves circulates through the complex veins of the vascular ring. The starch is deposited in special storage cells located in the area surrounding the ring. The interior of the potato, known as the **pith,** contains little starch or other nutrients. Its tissues are filled with large quantities of water.

24

Above: The outer layer of this potato has been cut away so that you can see the complicated veins of the vascular system, outlined by colored water. *Right:* A cross-section shows the potato's vascular ring.

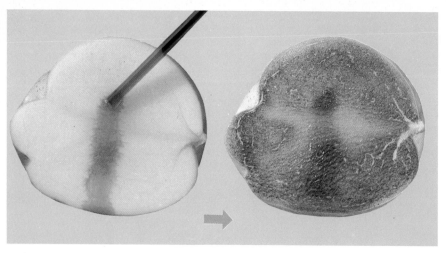

Iodine put on the cut surface of a potato reacts with starch to cause the potato's white flesh to darken.

You can see for yourself the starch stored in a potato tuber by performing a simple test with an ordinary cooking potato and a bottle of iodine from your bathroom medicine cabinet. Cut the potato in half and brush its cut surface with iodine. The iodine will quickly change the white flesh of the potato to a blue-black or blue-purple color.

This reaction is caused by the presence of starch in the potato cells. If you remember how the starch is stored in the tuber, you will not be surprised to see that the color is darkest around the edge and lightest at the center.

After you have done this experiment, take a look at the knife that you used to cut the potato. You should see a white powdery substance dried on the blade. This is the residue of the starch-filled water that oozed from the potato when you cut it. Like the color change caused by the iodine, it is evidence of the large amount of starch stored in a potato tuber.

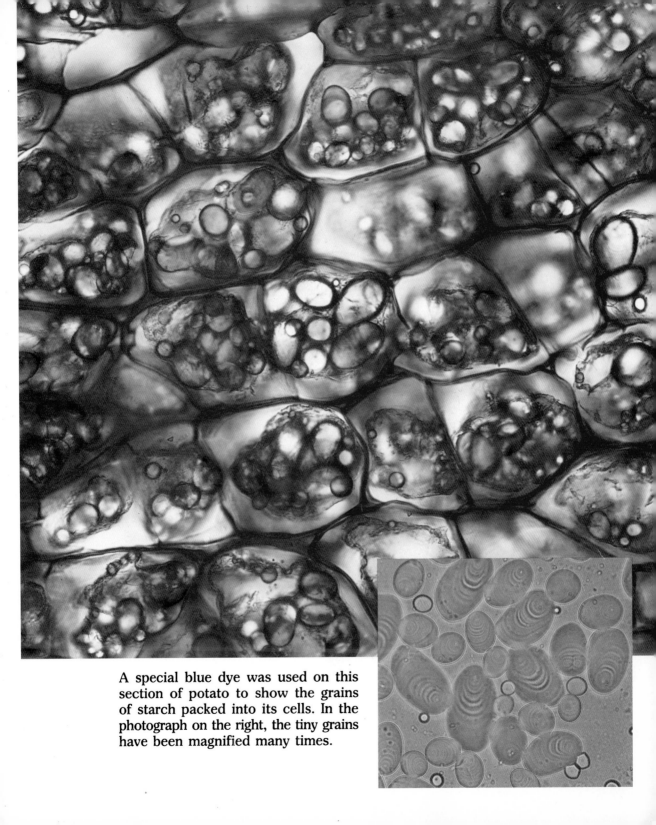

A special blue dye was used on this section of potato to show the grains of starch packed into its cells. In the photograph on the right, the tiny grains have been magnified many times.

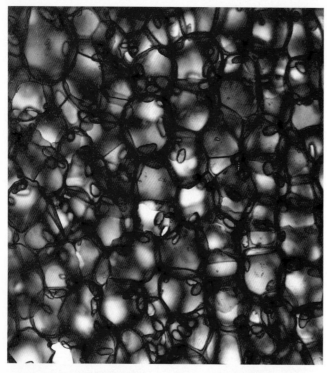

A seed potato's stored starch is used to provide energy for the the growth of the potato plant. The seed potato above, taken from the ground when the rhizomes first began to develop, still has some starch left in it. In the stained slide shown on the left, you can see a few blue starch grains in the potato's cells.

By the time the tubers have reached the size of ping-pong balls, all the starch in the seed potato has been used up. Iodine brushed on the potato does not produce a dark color (below), and there are no blue grains to be seen in the cells (left).

Some tubers on this potato plant have almost reached their full size, while others are just beginning to develop. The seed potato, its job done, is hollow and shriveled.

A potato plant's tubers begin to develop about five to seven weeks after planting. The tubers on one plant grow at different rates as each one receives its share of the plant's stored starch. The amount of moisture that the plant receives also affects the growth of the tubers. Potatoes need substantial amounts of water in order to develop large, evenly formed tubers. In areas without adequate rainfall, growers irrigate their potato fields to make sure that the plants get the necessary moisture.

During their period of growth, it is important that tubers be shielded from sunlight. Exposure to the sun causes them to become green and bitter. The hills of soil built up around potato plants protect the tubers growing near the surface from the damaging effects of sunlight.

The white flowers of
a potato plant open
their petals.

At the same time that the tubers are developing underground, flowers are beginning to appear on the tops of the potato plants. These delicate blossoms bring a touch of soft color to the intense green of the potato field.

The graceful potato flower may remind you of the flower of another common garden plant, the tomato. The two kinds of flowers are similar because potatoes and tomatoes are closely related. They are both members of the scientific family Solanaceae. Other familiar plants in this family are eggplant and tobacco.

The family Solanaceae also has some rather sinister members. Belladonna, or deadly nightshade, and jimson weed are both poisonous plants in this group. The leaves and stems of potato plants contain a poisonous substance too, but it is much less powerful than the poison of the potato's dangerous relatives.

30

A field of potato plants in flower

Above and below: **The flowers of two varieties of cultivated potatoes**

Potato flowers come in different colors, depending on the variety of the plant that produced them. Many varieties of cultivated potatoes have white flowers, while others bear blossoms in shades of lavender and pink. Potato plants that grow wild in South America and other parts of the world often have vividly colored purple flowers.

Wild potato plants often have brightly colored flowers.

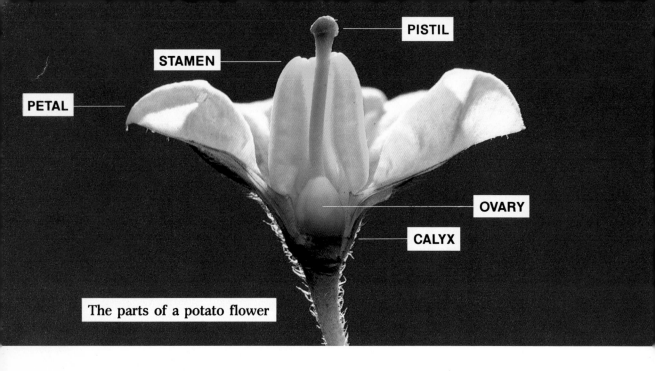

PISTIL

STAMEN

PETAL

OVARY

CALYX

The parts of a potato flower

Like the flowers of other kinds of green plants, the potato flower has a very important role. Its job is to produce seeds from which new plants can grow.

Seeds are formed through the process of **sexual reproduction,** and flowers contain the plant's male and female reproductive organs. The female organ of a flower is the **pistil,** a slender, tube-like structure with a sticky knob at the top. At the base of the pistil is the **ovary,** which contains tiny **ovules** that can develop into seeds.

Surrounding the pistil are five yellow **stamens,** the male organs of the potato flower. Stamens produce a fine, dust-like material called **pollen,** which contains sperm cells. When male sperm cells unite with female egg cells in the ovules, seeds begin to develop.

34

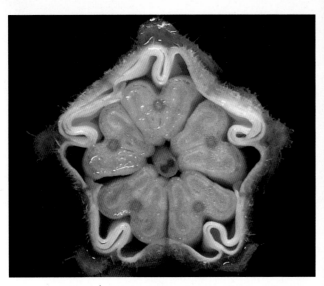

Above: This view from above shows the potato flower's five yellow stamens clustered around the pistil.

The pistil's sticky knob, called the stigma (center right), rises high above the stamens (upper right). This position makes it difficult for pollen produced by a flower to fall on its own pistil.

Tiny grains of pollen (below) are released through holes in the tips of the stamens (lower right).

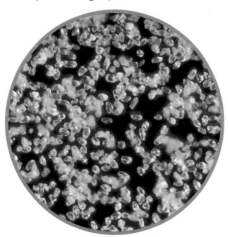

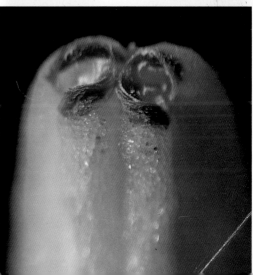

Insects such as this hover fly help to transfer pollen from one potato flower to another.

Like the flowers of most green plants, potato flowers are constructed in such a way that sperm cells and egg cells from the same flower cannot easily unite. In order for the flower to produce seeds, it usually receives pollen from the stamens of another flower. This transfer of pollen takes place with the help of insects that come to the potato flowers attracted by the sweet nectar they contain.

When an insect lands on a pollen-producing flower, it picks up pollen grains on its body and legs. It then carries these grains to other flowers, where they rub off on the sticky tips of the pistils. The grains of pollen split open, sending out tiny tubes that extend down through the stalk of the pistil into the ovary. Sperm cells move down the tubes to unite with the egg cells in the ovules, and seeds begin to develop.

36

Many plants are grown for their fruit, but the fruit of a potato plant (above) is not part of the human diet. The tubers (right) are the only part of the plant that is eaten.

After seeds begin to grow inside the ovary, the other parts of the potato flower wither and die. The ovary, however, changes to form a protective case around the growing seeds. It becomes a small, green **fruit** that looks very much like a cherry tomato.

Even if you grow potatoes in your backyard garden, you may have never seen a potato fruit. Many modern varieties of cultivated potatoes do not produce seeds or the fruits that enclose them. People don't eat potato fruits as they do the fruits of tomato, bean, pea, and numerous other kinds of garden plants. Potatoes are cultivated for their tubers, which grow without the presence of fruits, seeds, or even flowers. Potato seeds aren't even needed to produce new plants since potato plants grow easily from the tubers.

Potato fruits and seeds are not completely useless, however. As you will learn later, they play an important role in the creation of new potato varieties.

A field of potatoes ready for harvesting

When the flowers have bloomed and withered and the tubers are completely developed, it is time for harvesting. Growers find it easier to dig the tubers from the ground when the potato plants are dead. In areas where the harvest does not take place until late autumn, frost often kills the plants before growers are ready to put their equipment into the fields. When harvesting is done in spring or summer, chemicals may be used to destroy the stems and leaves of the potato plants when their job of producing tubers is finished.

Most large commercial growers harvest their potatoes with large machines that dig the tubers out of the ground, shake the dirt off them, and deposit them in trucks. Smaller potato producers often harvest by hand after using digging equipment to unearth the potatoes.

Above: Harvesting potatoes on the flat fields of the Red River Valley in the northern United States. *Below:* A mechanical potato harvestor digs potatoes up and separates them from the soil before depositing them in trucks.

Workers gather potatoes that have been unearthed by a potato digger.

After potatoes are harvested, they are sorted by size and condition. Some of the tubers are then shipped directly to markets or processors, but most are put into storage. They are placed in special warehouses with good ventilation, high humidity, and cool temperatures.

The temperature in potato warehouses is usually kept between 40 and 50 degrees Fahrenheit (4 to 10 degrees Celsius). At higher temperatures, the tubers might begin to sprout, while low temperatures will cause their stored starch to turn to sugar. (For this reason, it is not a good idea to keep potatoes in your refrigerator.)

Properly stored, potatoes can be preserved in good condition for as much as a year after harvesting.

Left: **Russet Burbank is the leading variety of potato grown in North America. It accounts for almost 40 percent of potatoes sold.** *Right:* **Norchip is a round potato developed for processing as chips.**

When potatoes are removed from storage, many of them are sold to processing plants, where they will be turned into potato chips, french fries, and countless other potato products. About 50 percent of the potatoes grown in the United States are used for processing rather than being sold fresh. This market is so important to American growers that special varieties of potatoes have been developed for the particular needs of processors. The Norchip potato (shown above), bred in the 1960s, is particularly suited for processing into chips. Other potato varieties make good french fries or dried potato flakes.

The leading variety grown in North America, the Russet Burbank, is a versatile potato used for many purposes. An excellent baking potato, it has a long, thin shape well suited for the french fries that are so popular with American consumers.

This red potato was developed at North Dakota State University during the 1970s. After several years of testing, the new variety was given the name Redsen and made available to growers in 1983.

The useful Russet Burbank originated from a potato variety developed in the 1870s by the famous American plant scientist Luther Burbank. Burbank created his new potato by experimenting with seeds.

Growing plants from seeds is the only way to get a new potato variety. If you plant a seed potato, you will get a **clone**—a plant exactly like the one that produced the seed potato. If you plant a potato *seed*, however, you will have a different plant with the combined characteristics of the two parent plants that formed the seed.

Today, plant scientists use the technique of cross-breeding to produce seeds for new varieties of potatoes. A scientist will choose two plants with desirable features and then transfer pollen from one plant to the pistils of the other. The seeds that result from this union will combine characteristics from both parent plants. After performing this experiment again and again, the scientist may eventually produce a new variety of potato with characteristics well

Under their brilliantly colored skins, these potatoes have the same white flesh as the more familiar brown-skinned varieties.

suited to the needs of growers. Seed potatoes from the new variety can then be used to produce exactly the same kind of plant in fields all over the world.

In North America, 80 percent of the potato crop is made up of only six different varieties. There are over 5,000 known varieties of potato, many of them very different in appearance from the familiar oval, brown-skinned Russet Burbank. Some varieties of potato grown in South America have twisted, knobby shapes and skins of deep purple, black, or violet.

43

South America is the original home of the cultivated potato, and the tubers have been grown there for centuries. When Spanish explorers arrived in Peru during the 1500s, they found the potato to be a staple crop of the mighty Inca Empire. The Incas ate potatoes fresh and used dried potatoes to make a kind of flour that could be kept for long periods of time without spoiling.

When the Spanish and other explorers introduced the potato to Europe in the 1500 and 1600s, the tuber was not immediately accepted as a food. Europeans were familiar with deadly nightshade and other poisonous plants in the family Solanaceae, and they associated potatoes with their dangerous relatives. Eventually, this reluctance was overcome, and potatoes became an important food crop in many European countries. When settlers from Europe came to North America, they brought the precious tubers with them.

Today, growers around the world produce around 290 million tons (261 million metric tons) of potatoes each year. Russia leads in the production of potatoes, growing about 33 percent of the world crop. Poland, the United States, and China are also major producers of the nutritious tubers.

Potatoes have come a long way from their origins in the small mountain fields of South America. Processed into chips and fries or eaten fresh, they have taken their place among the most popular of the world's foods.

GLOSSARY

buds—small plant structures that develop into stems, leaves, or flowers

chlorophyll (KLOR-uh-fil)—a green pigment that absorbs sunlight, producing the energy that makes photosynthesis possible

chloroplasts (KLOR-uh-plasts)—tiny bodies in plant cells that contain chlorophyll

clone (KLON)—a new plant or animal with exactly the same genetic make-up as the individual that produced it

compound leaves—plant leaves made up of separate sections or leaflets

eyes—small indentations on a potato that contain buds

fruit—the part of a plant that develops from the flower ovary and encloses the seeds

glucose (GLU-kose)—a form of sugar produced by plants during photosynthesis

leaflets—the individual sections of a compound leaf

ovary—the enlarged base of the pistil, which contains ovules

ovules (AHV-yuls)—tiny structures in a flower ovary that can develop into seeds

photosynthesis (fot-uh-SIN-thih-sis)—the process by which green plants use the energy of the sun to make food

pistil—the female reproductive organ of a flower

46

pith—the central portion of a potato tuber

pollen—the powdery substance produced by stamens, containing male sperm cells

rhizome (RI-zohm)—an underground portion of a stem

seed potatoes—potatoes planted in the soil in order to produce new potato plants

sexual reproduction—a form of reproduction in which a new individual is created by the union of male and female sex cells

stamens (STAY-muhns)—the male reproductive organs of a flower

starch—a substance built up of molecules of glucose, used to store food energy in plants

stomata (STO-muh-tuh)—the tiny pores or openings in plant leaves. The singular form of the word is **stoma.**

tuber (TYU-buhr)—an enlarged portion of a rhizome, used to store starch. The tuber is the part of the potato plant that we eat.

vascular (VAS-kyu-luhr) bundles—collections of tiny veins running through a plant stem. The veins carry water and food to all parts of the plant.

vascular ring—the ring-shaped pattern of veins seen in a cross-section of a plant stem or tuber

INDEX